Prayer AT FULL THROTTLE

Prayer AT FULL THROTTLE

How Performance-Based Prayers Make Miracles Happen

WRITTEN BY:

ROBERT BAKKE

authorHOUSE®

AuthorHouse™
1663 Liberty Drive
Bloomington, IN 47403
www.authorhouse.com
Phone: 1-800-839-8640

Published by AuthorHouse   04/01/2015

ISBN: 978-1-4918-1492-5 (sc)
ISBN: 978-1-4918-1491-8 (hc)
ISBN: 978-1-4918-1490-1 (e)

Library of Congress Control Number: 2013915893

Print information available on the last page.

Cover photo by: Rob Schrader Photography

To my friend, Jesus Christ.
You took the bullet that was intended for me.
It was an act of love that will never be forgotten.

CONTENTS

PUT AWAY THE PHD
(AN INTRODUCTION)

A FEW YEARS AGO I began reading a book about prayer. The book was so complicated, I became intimated and quit reading it. If a person has to become that theological before attempting to pray, then all of my prayers—and possibly yours!—have fallen null and void.

And that, my friends, is baloney.

Prayer is simply a heartfelt conversation between you and God. It is no more complicated than a child wanting to share their innermost thoughts, problems, and desires with his or her father, and no father requires a child to qualify in any way before allowing that to happen. Just as we love our children, God loves you, and He is listening to your every word when you pray.

It is after we have finished praying when most of us need enlightenment. This enlightenment comes in the form "earning" your blessing or miracle. While this thought might give a lot of theologians a toothache, the fact remains that we need to put action behind our prayer. If we don't engage in some kind of performance, our prayer blessing and our miracle is likely to remain in neutral. Let's not let that happen.

The book of James in the New Testament reveals that "faith without works is dead" (James 2:20). For some people, the word "works" is clear enough. For others, they relate to being "doers of the Word." Personally, I relate more easily to the words "corresponding action." But my favorite works-related term is the word "performance."

The word "performance" is used a mere 71 times in both the Old and New Testaments combined. Odds are you've never even noticed it. What I enjoy about this word is that according to the Strong's Exhaustive Concordance, the word "performance" used in its various contexts can be associated with the following terms: rise up, commit, endure, bring forth, accomplish, battle, finish, and succeed.

I've seen what happens when you rise up, commit, and finish your prayers with corresponding actions instead of sitting idly by waiting for answers. And I've got the pictures to prove it in the following pages. As you read through this book, you'll begin to see what I'm talking about. When your prayers are followed by performance, your prayer life will produce blessings and miracles unlike anything you have ever seen.

Faith Without Sweat, Is Dead

Get ready to bring your prayer life to an entirely new level. It is time, as odd as this may sound, to roll up your sleeves and put some sweat behind those prayers of yours. Remember, the Bible says that faith without works is *dead*. And so are prayers. So get ready to learn how prayers backed by performance on your part will produce tangible results, and even miracles, right here in the world in which you live. But before we go any further, there's a couple things you'll need to do.

First, you'll need to open the windows of your imagination and unshackle the *full power* of God's Word. Why do I say this? Because the sad fact is, most "Christians" have never taken the time to actually *read* the Bible, so they don't even know what God's Word says. Other Christians who have read it, pick and choose what they decide to believe, and then assemble their chosen bits and pieces into an imaginary god who doesn't even exist! Get real. Praying to an imaginary god will produce manifestations that are just as imaginary. No more! It is time to unleash the full-power, *full-throttle* Word of God in your life! That means reading, discussing and accepting *all* of the Bible's teachings, including those subjects that human intellect, ego and even *fears* have caused Christians to disregard. Subjects like faith healing, which many Christians dismiss even though Jesus healed people every day and said that you and I could perform even greater miracles if we would only believe! Praying in heavenly languages gets dismissed even though 1 Corinthians 13:1 is read at almost every wedding! Most Christians also avoid tithing by dismissing it as purely an Old Testament practice, which it isn't. And the "taking up" of the church gets dismissed even though 1Thessalonians 4:16-17 describes this as the most awesome event of them all! Look at it this way. If you want God to answer your prayers, you need to stop praying to your watered-down imaginary god, and start praying to the all-powerful real One. Sound reasonable? It is time to accept the full-gospel, *full-throttle* Word of God! Finally believing every Word of God to be true will produce the greatest thrill ride you have ever taken.

The second thing we need to do before we begin is called "erasing the chalkboard."

Imagine an old country schoolhouse. Within the four walls of the schoolhouse is a single classroom. On the front wall of the classroom is one of those old dusty chalkboards. Can you picture it? Good. This is where you need to pay attention. Written on this old dusty chalkboard is the name of every person who has ever done you wrong. Everyone who has ever lied to you, stolen from you, cheated on you or hurt your feelings. Take your time with this so every possible name of every possible person appears on the chalkboard. Then take *one last look* at every one of these names so this exercise fully sinks in.

Now, imagine picking up an eraser and erase every name you see written on the chalkboard. Do it! This is called *forgiveness*. Mark 11:25 instructs us to forgive before we pray, so erasing the chalkboard becomes a necessary first step.

Next, imagine coming into the classroom with a bucket of water, a sponge and a drying towel. Imagine sponging down the chalkboard with water and then drying the chalkboard with a fresh, clean towel. This is called *forgetting*.

You have now learned to *forgive and forget*, which as you know is *divine*. By erasing your chalkboard, you and your heart are now in a perfect position from which to pray. So let's get started.

What exactly is a *performance-based* prayer? It is a prayer that is supported by *corresponding action*. Too many people have become derailed by the phrase "waiting on the Lord." Basically, they have turned praying and waiting into praying and *sitting*. Performance-based prayer is the exact opposite of praying and sitting. Performance-based prayer means "praying and *performing*." It is about getting to work and *earning* your miracle. How do I know this type of prayer produces results? Because of the prayer blessings and manifestations that appear in my life almost every day. Blessings that I will share with you as we go along and that will increase the strength of your own prayer expectations.

My personal walk of faith has been quite a journey. It has taken me from being the skinny, insecure little kid who was picked last in gym class every day to the blessings of racing NASCAR, flying jet airplanes and even a black belt in Shotokan karate. These blessings and the obedient endurance they required are significant on a number of levels. First, because they've resulted in a lifestyle that is far outside the lines of the mainstream image of what a Christian lifestyle looks like. This benefits the Lord because it makes people sit up and take notice! Remember, we Christians are supposed to let our lights shine! That means living a life so bright and exciting that others see something in us that they want for themselves! Can you think of a better way to inspire God's children to come home to their Father? But that won't happen as long as Christians accept the misguided teaching that we are to live quietly in the shadows like passive little church mice. It is time for Christians to click their lights back on . . . to put their gifts to use and perform at levels that non-Christians will thirst for! It is imperative that we cement this into our thinking and into our actions. We have the power of God in us! We are *instructed* to glorify the Lord through our good works! That means doing more than just talking. It means *performing*. And performing at the highest of levels.

Secondly, the blessings I've received through performance-based prayer provide undeniable evidence of physical manifestation. These blessings prove what can happen when you mix corresponding action with your faith. Make no mistake, when you pray and perform, supernatural things will happen. Period.

Finally and perhaps most significantly, these blessings show how the outcome of our prayers are influenced by living the life we were created to live . . . by *getting to work* and living the life we were *designed and built for*. Living this way requires both courage and obedience and is far more powerful than most people realize. Unfortunately, it is a life that few people live.

In a survey of hospice patients that was released in 2012, it was revealed that the number one regret of a hospice patient (someone who is dying) was that they wished they would have had the courage to live a life true to themselves and not the life others expected of them. This is sad beyond description and a revelation that we all need to learn from! The study revealed that most people, and probably even yourself, have a feeling deep down that life was intended to be something different than what it is. You *must* pay attention to this. A hospice patient is out of options, but you aren't! Yes, life can be filled with obstacles and distractions, but you must find the courage to accept what God created you to be, and then put some sweat into it! Because as you will see, the manifestation of your prayers will be significantly enhanced when you finally decide to become the real you.

FISH DON'T CLIMB TREES

WHEN IT COMES TO being the real you, perhaps a bit of comedy from Albert Einstein will help show you the way. Albert Einstein once wrote, "Everybody is a genius. But if you judge a fish by its ability to climb a tree, it will live its whole life believing it is stupid."

Consider the problems, challenges and difficulties that a fish would encounter while trying to live on land. The fish would quickly discover climbing trees is the least of its worries. It would have trouble with its mobility, trouble finding food, trouble drinking water, and trying to breathe would be nearly impossible. Just imagine the frustrations and health issues the fish would be suffering from! The poor little fish would be praying up a storm! "Please, Father, help me with my mobility. Please, Father, help me to find water to drink. Please, Father, help me to find food to eat and air to breathe. Please, Father, heal my body." But, if the fish would just get back into the water where it belongs, all of its problems would be solved! All of its prayers and cries for help would be answered just by following God's plan for its life! Can a fish still have problems underwater? Sure, it can. But a fish is better equipped to handle the problems that occur underwater than the problems that occur on land. And because the fish is being obedient to God's plan, you can bet God will respond to its prayers more quickly and with more fervency.

So many people struggle trying to discover God's purpose for their life. But it's not that difficult once you learn how to recognize it. We'll talk a little about this now, and then cover it in more detail a bit later.

For most people, their purpose for being here has been in their minds since childhood. It's been there like a heavenly GPS trying to point them in the right direction; they just haven't recognized it for what it was. What I'm telling you is, pay attention to your mind and the mental images that appear within your imagination. Most specifically, those images that bring you feelings of joy! Give merit to the pictures that put a twinkle in your eye and a smile on your face! Do this, and soon you'll begin to feel a "burning desire." This is usually the sign that God is trying to move you in a specific direction. I say "usually" because a person has to qualify why they're excited. If your excitement is based on lust, greed or some other attribute with origins in darkness, obviously your visions are not from the enlightenment of God. They need to be disregarded. Conversely, a God-given vision is in alignment with the talents and abilities God has blessed you with. You can bet it wasn't God who told the fish to leave the water and climb a tree. God would never give you a burning desire for something without giving you the skills to achieve it! That would be setting you up to fail, and God isn't in that business. God-given visions are designed to point you in the direction of God's purpose for your life. Once you've accepted this and have aligned your goals with God's plan for your life, a synergy between you and God is created, and in the world of prayer, this becomes extremely powerful!

Let me share an example.

People often ask if I'm ever afraid of getting hurt in my racecar. Worse yet, they ask if I'm afraid of getting *killed* in the airplane. My answer is always the same, "Never." The reason for this is simple. Before every race, with my safety harness buckled and the racecar's engine running, I say a prayer. I say a prayer thanking God for the ability to race automobiles. I ask that He keeps me safe, and that He helps me to race fast and clean and honor Him in all that I do. I pray a similar prayer before flying the jet. I thank Him for the ability to fly airplanes, and ask Him to keep myself and the passengers safe. When we're flying in bad weather, I pray again, asking God to actually "keep the airplane in the palm of His hands." Having said these prayers, whether I'm in the racecar or in the jet, I know in my heart that myself, and my passengers, will remain safe. The secret behind this is that I also know in my heart that I am following God's plan for my life, and God would never allow me to be harmed while doing something He has created me to do. Being enlightened to this produces the confidence to speak prayers with unshakable faith. When you have faith this strong, your prayers produce unlimited horsepower. But to pray with a true and confident expectation of an outcome is something not all Christians are doing. For an example of this, let's consider the prayers of my friend, Jenny.

Jenny is a Christian who works as a dental hygienist. During my last dental visit, I mentioned to her that I was writing this message on "prayer." I went on to explain how I wanted to help build a faith so strong in people that when they prayed over something, they could step back and literally watch the changes occur. At this point, Jenny was staring at me with a look of skepticism, to which I replied, "I have photographic evidence to prove it can happen."

Jenny responded with a soft voice, "I guess when I pray . . . I pray and doubt."

"How's that been working for you?" I replied with a grin on my face.

"Not very well," she replied.

Jenny had failed to remember some of the scriptures found in the New Testament. Scriptures such as

Matthew 9:29, in which Jesus says, "According to your faith be it unto you." Or in James 1:6-8, where we're told to "Ask in faith, never doubting, for the one who doubts must not expect to receive anything from the Lord." A person should never pray with doubt! It is an insult to God, particularly to a God who is "Almighty."

Unfortunately, while many Christians may not admit it like Jenny did, too many Christians share her same thoughts and prayer habits. They pray and they doubt, which is the farthest thing from praying with faith. This practice has no basis in scripture whatsoever, and will only lead to prayers that go unanswered.

Praying with doubt is not how God wants us to be seeking His help! Think about it. How would *you* feel if one your own children came to you needing help, but deep down, they believed you either wouldn't help them or that you were incapable of helping them? Would it hurt your feelings? Would you be disappointed that your child doesn't believe you? Of course you would. When we *pray and doubt*, it makes God feel the same way. I'll tell you how I know this in the paragraphs to come. But in the meantime, try putting some thought into aligning *your* goals with God's!

Apparently, God Drives a Ford?

Praying and doubting has to stop. To help make that happen, let's start thinking about prayer in terms of a *spectrum*. We'll call one end of the spectrum, "praying and doubting." We'll call the other end, "praying and believing." Our mission today is to take you on a journey from one end of the spectrum to the other, making praying and *doubting* a thing of the past and praying and *believing* (a performance-based practice), the way of the future.

As we begin our journey through prayer, there's something we need to eliminate right from the start. That *something* is the first of some clichés that have crept into our speech patterns. The first of these clichés is the one that refers to how we've been "created in God's image." To be clear, I'm talking specifically about the cliché and not about the *teaching*. In fact, today more than ever, we need to accept and believe that we are in fact created in God's image! But as you're about to learn, this reference to "image" goes far beyond the limitation of just our physical appearance. It was the limitation to *physical appearance* that caused the cliché in the first place, which is why a deeper examination of this teaching is required.

When God created us in His image, the design went far beyond what most people take time to consider. This reference to "image" refers to much more than just our physical bodies. In 2 Peter 1:4, we learn that we also share God's "divine nature." Let that sink in a minute. That means we also resemble God with our emotional and intellectual levels as well. We share His ability to think and to make decisions. In the Old Testament book of Isaiah, we learn we share God's ability to *reason*. We also know that God feels joy, just as we feel joy, and that God even laughs! Can you imagine? God laughs? It makes me want to tell Him my best jokes just to see what He'll do! Can you imagine God sitting on His throne in heaven just cracking up, slapping His knee, laughing so hard He's got tears coming down His cheeks? Wow, there's a sight!

Along with His laughter, we also know that God feels anger, just as we feel anger, and that God spoke the universe into existence with the sound waves of His voice, just as you and I have voice. A voice that creates sound waves that we know can break glass! Fascinating . . . isn't it?

Understanding the similarities of how we think, laugh, reason and react just as God does provides insight into how our behavior here on earth affects our relationship with God, and subsequently, affects the outcome of our prayers.

The first situation that opened my eyes to this occurred back in the 1980s. It was just after I bought my first pick up truck, a Ford F150 half-ton. Granted, today there are sport utility vehicles parked in almost every driveway. But living in the suburbs back in the '80s, if you owned a pickup truck, you had the only utility vehicle for miles around. Herein lies the first lesson in how relationships can impact your prayer life.

During the years I owned that first truck, I used to receive phone calls that, even though the names would change, the calls were pretty much the same. They sounded something like this:

"Ring, ring . . ."

Me: "Hello?"

Tim: "Hi Robert!"

Me: "Hi. Umm. Who is this?"

Tim: "Tim . . . Tim Johnson, from the softball team. Tall, thin, blonde hair. I play right field."

Me: "Oh, sure. Hi, Tim, how are you?

Tim: "Good."

Me: "What's up?"

Tim: "Nothing really, just wanted to say hello. How have you been?"

Me: "Okay."

Tim: "How's the job going?"

Me: "Good."

Tim: "Still skiing?"

Me: "Yep."

Uncomfortable pause . . .

Me: "What's new with you?"

Tim: "Oh . . . not much. The job is okay. Cathy is good. Although we rented a new apartment, and you know what a hassle *moving* can be."

Me: "Yep. Sure do."

Another uncomfortable pause . . .

Tim: "Say, ah, you still got that truck?"

Bingo! There's your first lesson in prayer! Christians are making too many calls to God the way guys like Tim made calls to me! They only call God when they need Him for something! Don't even *try* to tell me you haven't done this, because I've done it myself. We all have. Sure, I knew God was out there, but it took buying a Ford F150 to finally open my eyes to the fact I only called God when I needed Him for something! In the situation with Tim, if he and I were in regular fellowship, I would have already known about his upcoming move and would have "blessed him" with the use of my truck before he even asked to borrow it! There's a big lesson in this, and I hope it's sinking in.

Calling people only when we need to "use them for something" is not a good pathway to fellowship. We don't like it, and neither does God. How do we know God doesn't like it? Because you and I are created in God's image and nature, and we don't like it either! Plus, it leads to the same old answer that none of us like to hear. That answer is "no."

Thank the Lord
for Taco Bell!

As sad as it is, we've just confirmed there are people who will only acknowledge you as a friend when they need you for something. These people are *not* friends, and they are not givers. They are *takers*. They are not producers; they are *consumers*. Acting this way with God and only praying to Him when we need Him for something is not going to get our prayers answered when or how we want them to be answered.

When it comes to prayer, we need to keep our focus on Bible scriptures like 1 John 3:22 that states, "Whatsoever we ask of Him, we receive because we keep His commandments." You might want to let that sink in a minute, because in Mark 12:30, the first commandment says, "Thou shall love the Lord your God with all thy heart, and with all thy soul, and with all thy mind, and all thy strength." Only praying to God when you need Him for something certainly doesn't meet that criteria. The Bible says that we are to seek God first! Calling God only when we need Him for something isn't keeping Him number one. It is keeping Him number *last!*

For our prayers to begin showing signs of increased power, we must commit to seeking and keeping God first in our lives. Hebrews 11:6 tells us that "God is a rewarder of those who *diligently* seek Him." But what does that look like? How do we do it? Where do we start? It begins each day when you turn off your alarm clock and speak the words, "Good morning God!" and do it first thing in the morning.

Next, before you turn on the television, open the newspaper or log on to the internet, open your Bible and read God's Word *first.* And if you can, read it *out loud.* Romans 10:17 tells us that "Faith comes by hearing, and hearing by the Word of God." Reading out loud, even to yourself, gives you the chance to "hear" God's Word, and faith comes by hearing! So do this! And do it first thing, because God's Word is far more important than anything that shows up in the morning news! Trust me, the morning news can wait. Furthermore, for your prayers to be fully effectual, they need to be *in agreement* with God's Word. But how can your prayers be in agreement with God's Word if you don't know what God's Word says! So read it!

Finally, before you start sending emails or talking on your cell phone, communicate with God through prayer *first*. Have a conversation with Him. Fellowship with Him each morning. Yes, I realize you'll need to visit with your spouse and children as morning obligations require. However, before having your first longwinded conversation with a coworker about what's going on at the office, have a conversation with God *first!*

Talking to God doesn't always have to be a formal prayer event. You can talk to God while you're driving to work in your car. You can even turn your car into a "Rolling University" by loading your car with Christian CDs and listening to them on the way to work and back. You'll be amazed at the Bible teachings you can receive during your daily commute! And again, remember that Romans 10:17 says, "Faith comes by hearing and hearing!" Your daily commute is an excellent way to accomplish this. Plus, being alone in your car is an awesome time to communicate with God.

Look at it this way. Consider how much time we *don't* spend communicating with God. Be honest, how many minutes a day do you spend in prayer? How many minutes a day do you spend talking to everyone else? And what about this: How many books are in your home right now? Take a moment and think about it. How many different school books, romance novels, professional manuals and sports magazines are currently scattered around your house? Several, correct? How many of these publications do you glance through on a regular basis? I'll tell you how many. Lots of them. You flip through so many different books and magazines I bet you have trouble remembering them all.

Now for the painful questions. How many Bibles do you have in your home? Have you ever actually read the Bible? Come on, really? Cover to cover? Because most of the people who say they've read the Bible haven't. The fact is, we can be so remiss about spending time in God's Word, or diligently seeking Him, that it borders on inexcusable. If we ever want to experience the true power of prayer, this obviously needs to change.

So, while it was the purchase of a Ford F150 that originally opened my eyes to the "relationship of convenience" that I had created with God, it was the relationship with my little godson that tore things wide open.

I have a godson named Robby. Robby was born to a struggling single mom who was raising two children on her own. As you can imagine, the expenses of day-to-day living had kept things pretty tight financially for her and her children.

As time passed and Robby had reached the age of eleven, he began looking to me as a father figure. He began "diligently seeking" for us to spend more time together. Not having a son of my own, this new relationship sank deeply into my heart, and I began providing for Robby more than ever before. It felt so good to finally have someone to provide for, and Robby was always so thankful for the things I would do for him. If I picked Robby up after school and took him to look at snowmobiles, then to a movie, and then to Taco Bell for dinner, it never failed . . . when I dropped Robby off at his mother's house, he would get out of the car and say, "Thank you for taking me to look at snowmobiles, and thank you for taking me to a movie, and thank you for taking me to Taco Bell." He was the most thankful person I had ever known, and he brought me more joy than I can find words to explain. I absolutely fell in love with doing things for him. So much so, that people began to suggest that I might be spoiling him. But my response was always the same, "When Robby stops thanking me, I'll stop giving."

It felt wonderful to give, and it felt even better knowing it was appreciated! And then it hit me. Everything that I had done for Robby was a "drop in the bucket" compared to what God had been doing for me. But how often was I saying "thank you" to God? And how often had I been diligently seeking Him? Not nearly enough. And there's the lesson we all need to learn from this.

How often are we diligently seeking and saying "thank you" to God?

We all need to wake up to the joy God feels when we do these things!

How do we know God enjoys it when we treat Him like this? Because you and I are created in God's image and nature, and we enjoy it when people treat us like this!

A Christmas Lesson
on "Praise"

MY GODSON SURE TAUGHT me a lot about my relationship with God. But then there was the day the clouds parted and I truly "saw the light." It happened during the Christmas season and it went something like this . . . .

With Christmas rapidly approaching I asked Robby what he was hoping to find under the Christmas tree. I wanted to know the one gift he *really* wanted. You know the gift I'm talking about. The "sky is the limit" gift. But when I asked him about the gift, Robby stood quiet and reserved, acting almost ashamed to ask for the toy that was truly on his heart.

It took a bit of prodding, but Robby eventually explained the details of a little remote control car he was hoping Santa would bring him. It was a yellow 1967 Chevrolet Impala with a bright red stripe. By the look on his face, there was no doubt this was the one gift he *really* wanted for Christmas, and I was determined to get it for him. Unfortunately, I would quickly learn how difficult it is to find a popular toy just one day before Christmas! It took multiple phone calls and more miles of driving than I care to remember, but eventually, payola! I finally found a store that had one! I bought the car, then got it wrapped and under the tree in time for Robby to find on Christmas morning.

Christmas morning arrived. Robby was thrilled to find the little yellow car he had wanted so badly. Robby went quickly into his mother's garage, raised the door, and began driving his new little car all around the garage and out onto the driveway. Just a few minutes later a couple of Robby's friends came walking by. Robby stopped his car, picked it up, and ran out to the street to show it to his friends. As he slowed to a stop, Robby cradled the car in one arm, and pointing back into the garage with the other, he shouted, "Look what Robert gave me!"

In that moment my relationship with the Lord changed forever. Because instead of Robby just giving me "thanks" as he does when I take him to Taco Bell, he had now demonstrated a higher level of appreciation called *praise*. This was the first time I had ever noticed what "praise" even looks like! Much less *feels* like or even *sounds* like. Look at it this way. When Robby gave me praise in front of his friends, he was giving praise to his godfather, who is "on earth," just as we are to give praise to our heavenly Father, who is "in heaven." Get it? (You might want to read that again.) It was at that instant I realized just how many blessings—tens of thousands of them—that I had failed to praise God for!

Please understand, the same little boy who taught me how to diligently seek and give *thanks* to my Father in heaven had now taught me to give *praise* to my Father in heaven. And now, he has taught you!

It felt really good to be given praise! And you can be assured that God enjoys it too! Do you know why? Because you and I are created in God's image and nature, and if we enjoy it, He enjoys it also!

ARE YOUR GIFTS STILL UNDER THE TREE?

TRY TO IMAGINE HOW many things we've failed to appreciate, or even worse yet, that we've taken credit for! Things like test scores, physical health, promotions at work, trophies on a shelf, beautiful children, just to name a few. You have to wonder, does our taking credit for the blessings we've received make God want to bless us more or bless us less? I'll let you answer that one for yourself.

This is all so simple, yet it took my eleven-year-old godson to get me to see it! Thank God for Robby! Through his example, my life changed forever. But, for the sake of perspective, let's look at it another way. Suppose Robby *wasn't* so thankful? Suppose he never thanked me for anything, and the gifts I had given him just sat in the corner gathering dust? Would I have been so generous? No way.

Think about it. Let's say you're a father and you have two sons. One of your sons is always joyful and pleasant. He is always appreciative, and whenever you bless him with a gift, he fills with excitement and uses it every day! He even goes outside and tells his buddies what a great dad he has. But then there is the other son, who is the complete opposite. The other son doesn't thank you for anything, never uses the gifts you give him and would certainly never consider praising you in front of his friends. Now ask yourself, if one of these two sons asked you for something beyond what you've already given them, which son are you most likely to respond to? I'll let you answer this one also.

Now let's ask a more difficult question. What has happened to the gifts and talents God has given *you?* Are you using them? Are you glorifying God with them? Are you competing and winning trophies with them? And if so, are you telling people about the God who gave them to you, or are you hogging all the credit for yourself? I know these are difficult and humbling questions, but before you can expect God to give you any additional gifts, doesn't it make sense that you should be using the gifts He has already given you? Just like a child with a gift under the Christmas tree, we should be popping the bows, snapping the ribbons, tearing off the paper and using our gifts until they're wearing out and falling apart! Think I'm kidding? I dare you to get up off the couch and step onto the field of battle. I dare you to put your talents and abilities to use and see for yourself how God's favor begins to show up in your life.

Just like you enjoy seeing your children using the gifts you have given them, God enjoys seeing you do the exact same thing. So get up, and get moving!

How do I know God enjoys seeing us using our gifts? Because you and I are created in His image and nature, and we enjoying seeing our children using theirs! Feeling a little intimidated? Um . . . good!

Your Body Is a Temple . . . for Real!

THERE'S SOMETHING ELSE YOU need to know about the gifts you've been given. Not only should you be using your gifts, but you should be taking care of them.

Never has a gift been overlooked, neglected and abused like the gift of the human body. Most people, most Christians, have long taken their bodies for granted. Think I'm kidding? Look around you. Look in the mirror. Perhaps step on a scale. The current state of fitness is America borders on obscene. We've gotten too comfortable watching everyone else fall away from fitness and then following their example, when in reality, we should have kept our attention on scripture.

Too many people have forgotten that 1 Corinthians 6:19 teaches that our bodies are the temple of the Holy Spirit. We are taught, no, *warned*, that if there is one gift we need to be taking care of, it's this one! If you check out Deuteronomy 21:20, you'll find that in the Old

Testament days, people were *stoned to death* for getting drunk and for overeating. Can you imagine what would happen today if we stoned people to death based on that standard? With the current amount of alcohol consumption and obesity in America, our population would suffer a significant decline. And don't get snared by thinking the book of Deuteronomy is Old Testament and we're "out from under the curse of the law." Fast forward into the New Testament and read 1 Corinthians 3:16-17 (First Corinthians was written in approximately 56 A.D.). I particularly enjoy the translation of these verses found in the New Revised Standard Version. It states: "Do you not know that you are God's temple and that God's Spirit dwells in you? If anyone destroys God's temple, God will destroy that person. For God's temple is holy, and you are that temple." If these verses don't get your attention, nothing will. Now I realize there will be those of you who say that according to some translations, these verses refer to the church body as a whole. I get that. But if you check the Amplified, you'll find it says that these verses include both the collective body of the church as well as you yourself "individually." Additionally, 1 Corinthians 6:19 will again confirm your body is the temple of the Holy Spirit. But, even with all that being said, there will be people who think none of this matters because we are now under "grace." This is true. We believers are under grace, but you still need to change your thinking. Even though we are under grace, that doesn't mean we should have to use it! The gift of grace wasn't intended to be a "get out of jail free" card that you can take reckless advantage of. That being said, read the scripture one more time. It does not say, "If it weren't for grace, God would destroy that person." The scripture says, "God *will* destroy that person." I know that sounds harsh, but did it get your attention? I hope so. The bottom line? Your body is a gift you need to be caring for.

So what does this mean to a person's prayer life? It's simple. If you are smoking cigarettes, drinking alcohol, overeating, using drugs or failing to exercise, whether individually or any combination of these, you are not caring for your gift of the temple. Failing to care for such a precious gift and then asking God for something more is a request that will go unanswered. Imagine someone filling their temple with cigarette smoke, alcohol and fattening foods and then asking God for a healing? It happens every single day, and every single day, a prayer goes unanswered.

Not to sound totally grim, a person not caring for their temple can find themselves surrounded by advantages, because they have so many opportunities to put *works* into their faith. For example, they can pray for their health and *quit smoking*, which is *works*. They can pray for their health and quit drinking, which is *works*. They can pray for their health and stop overeating, which is *works*. They can pray for their health and start exercising, which is *works*. You could begin a diet, which is *works*. For this person, the opportunity for performance-based prayer abounds! And prayers, backed by performance, produce miracles!

Your body is the temple of the Holy Spirit. It is God's temple, and is as great a gift as you can ever receive. Treat your body like the treasure it is, and maybe that next prayer request will receive the consideration you've been believing for.

Money: the True Test of Faith

So FAR THIS HAS been pretty easy stuff, don't you think? It's been like, "Relationship Basics 2.0." But now it's time to take it up a few notches. If you really want to see some power get behind those prayers of yours, you need to stop clinging to your cash, saddle up on your faith, and start *tithing.*

I'll forewarn you, I'm taking a hard line on this . . . so be ready.

Tithing is where the rubber meets the road. It is what separates the "Sunday morning Christian" from the real deal. Tithing differentiates the talkers from the doers, but handled incorrectly, it remains a subject that can drive "people of faith" away from a church quicker than any other subject in the Bible.

So many Christians profess they cannot worship both God and money, but yet they will get up and leave their church whenever the pastor even mentions this subject! If you are one of these Christians, I'm just curious . . . "How have your prayers been working?"

I thought so. So let's get into this.

For many Christians, just the mention of the word "tithing" can produce the tug of Satan himself. Maybe you feel it right now? Yep, that's him. He's already put a knot in your stomach. Do you feel it? That is the presence of the devil himself. The upside to the way you feel right now is that it *proves* to you Satan exists! But even though he exists, that doesn't mean he has to control you. And he certainly doesn't have to control your money, which by the way, is one of the ways he controls most people.

Many Christians excuse themselves from tithing by declaring it to be an Old Testament practice somehow only connected to the law. These rationalizations can be easily overturned by using the New Testament itself. First of all, you can find Jesus Himself making references to tithing in Matthew 23:23 and Luke 18:12. Secondly, there are substantial teachings about Abraham paying tithes to Melchizedek found in Hebrews 7:1-15. Additionally, in Galatians 3:17, you'll see that the law didn't come into existence until 430 years after God made His convenant with Abraham. That means Abraham and the practice of tithing was well under way before the law came into existence, so obviously, tithing is independent of the law.

When you find the strength to let go of your money, you break the grip of one of Satan's most powerful tools. But if you still think you can't afford to tithe, the following verse may help you begin to think otherwise.

Christians everywhere need to read Malachi 3:11. In this verse we are taught specifically that tithing will "rebuke the devourer." The devourer is Satan. The devil himself, who comes to steal, to kill and to destroy! He will destroy your job, your marriage, your home, your car and even your washing machine. It is what he lives for. The more he can destroy, the more he weakens your faith. Tithing rebukes this. The result of tithing is that your job will be more secure, your marriage will more secure and as crazy as it sounds, don't be surprised if your car and yes, even your washing machine are breaking down less often. Additionally, your tithe is tax deductible, so it even gives you a break on your taxes! The bottom line? The security and benefits that tithing provides will more than save you the cost of the tithing itself. If you don't believe this, you are calling God a liar. I'll let you take that up with Him.

Let's look at tithing on a prayer level. If you are a *non-tithing* Christian and your prayers seem to go unanswered, be careful not to blame God. And stop being upset with your pastor every time he tries to teach on the subject! Because if a subject is in the Bible, a pastor has the right, no, the *obligation* to teach it! And since the Bible gives instruction on the supernatural economy, getting upset with your pastor for teaching it is to become hostile with the Word of God itself! Getting hostile with God's Word will not get your prayers answered. Personally, I'd get upset with a pastor who *wasn't* teaching the subject of tithing! But that's me. I'm a Christian who believes in the full and uncompromised Word of God. This is something I wish for everyone.

Here's another way to look at tithing. God owns the earth and everything on it. This is His house, and as long as we live in God's house, we must live by God's rules. This is no different than telling your own children that as long as they live in *your* house, they have to live by *your* rules!

Get it?

But because so many "Christians" worship their money more than they worship God, their pastors continue to shy away from talking about money for fear they will lose their congregations. So here's the deal. *Christians* need to loosen the grip on their money, and *pastors* need to get stronger when it comes to teaching about it. Besides, if the subject of tithing was to actually cause a congregation to decline, the remaining members who see the light and begin tithing themselves will more than make up for any financial contraction. God will see to this because He blesses those who play by His rules. So ask yourself, would you rather give 10% of your money to your church and have God bless the remaining 90%, or keep all your money for yourself and have 100% of your money unblessed? Decide for yourself, but I'm willing to bet that a congregation who has 90% of their money blessed becomes a congregation who comes out ahead. Furthermore, the book of Galatians 6:7-9 makes it very clear that a person's harvest in life is dependent upon what they "sow." Providing financially for your church allows you to attach yourself to the "sowing" of God's Word into people's hearts. Rest assured that come harvest time, there will have been no better place for you to have sown your finances than into your chosen church or ministry. I cannot stress this enough.

It doesn't take a rocket scientist to see that the refusal to tithe is a significant misstep in a person's life of faith. Clinging to your money shows God you don't trust Him. Without trust, you cannot possibly "pray and believe." It simply cannot happen. So go ahead, be the believer you profess to be, and let God take control of your money. No offense, but He's better with it than you are!

EXPECT WHAT YOU DESERVE

A PERSON MUST UNDERSTAND that supernatural increase and prayer blessings are *not* an entitlement program. They require *works.* As we've just discussed, one of the ways we show God our *works* is by honoring Him with our tithes. By doing this, the Bible says God will bless us with increase. In fact, we can be so confident about this increase that God actually allows us to challenge Him on it! In the book of Malachi (3:10), we're told to bring all our tithes to the storehouse, and to "PROVE ME NOW," says the Lord of hosts, "if I will not open you the windows of heaven and pour you out a blessing, that there shall not be room enough to receive it." This is the only place in the scriptures I know where the Lord actually dares us to challenge Him on a teaching. One of the translations of this scripture says it this way: "Put me to the *test*, saith the Lord . . . ," again, challenging us to prove Him wrong that He will not pour us out a blessing! But for this to happen, we need to remember we are living in God's house, and when living in someone else's house, we must play by their rules!

Let's look at this in a way we can all relate to.

When I was young and needed money, I went to my dad and asked if he'd "float me some cash." My dad usually responded with something like, "If you're expecting me to give you some money there are a few things you'll need to do first. The lawn needs to be mowed, the garage needs to be cleaned and the car needs to be washed. Get this done, *first*, and we'll talk."

"But, Dad!" I'd reply, as though that somehow seemed unfair.

"My house, my rules," Dad would say.

The reality was, I knew if I wanted money for the weekend and maybe even a car to drive, I better do everything he asked me to do. The good news was, after I had done everything my father asked me to do, *first*, I could go back to him with a confident expectation of receiving what I had asked him for. Conversely, if I didn't play by the rules and failed to do what he had asked of me, I'd find myself sitting home with no money to spend and no car to drive. I didn't like it very much, but there was nothing unfair about it. In fact, when a parent gives a child something they don't deserve, it's referred to as "spoiling" the child. My father was extremely generous to me, but he never did anything to spoil me. You can rest assured that God, the ultimate Father, won't do anything to spoil you either.

We should never be expecting things we don't deserve. Not from God and not from anyone. So when God tells us to tithe before He pours out a blessing, it only makes sense that we do what He is asking. It's no different than having to pay for an item on a store shelf *before* you take it home with you. It's just the way things work.

Perhaps the most powerful teaching on tithing occurs in Malachi 3:8. It's here that we learn we're actually *stealing* from God by not tithing. Malachi 3:8-9 says, "Will a man rob God? Yet you have robbed me! But you say, In what way have we robbed you? *In tithes and offerings.* You are cursed with a curse, for you have robbed me . . . ."

If my effort to teach you about prayer at full throttle does nothing else, at least it has provided you with this one revelation. Well, this one revelation and perhaps the one that follows.

The Bible reveals different categories of behavior and disobedience. First, there are the lesser categories that I like to call the "flee and avoids." For example, we are instructed to "flee" from fornication. We are also told to "avoid" drunkenness. But in addition to the "flee and avoids," there are some higher levels of behavior and disobedience that are found in the Ten Commandments.

Or what I like to call "The Top-Ten." The ultimate "Thou shall, thou shall nots!"

As you read the commandments, you will find one that says, "Thou shall not steal." What's so powerful about this commandment against stealing is that it's on the same list that says, "Thou shall not *kill*."

THINK about that. Stealing and killing are on the same list! That being the case, what makes anyone think they can steal from God and then expect Him to respond to their prayer request? It makes no sense. That's like having a brother-in-law who steals your tools and then asks to borrow your truck! "Not today my brother. Stop stealing my tools and maybe I'll think about it."

First John 3:22 tells us that "Whatsoever we ask, we receive of Him, *because we keep His commandments* . . . ." To put it bluntly, not tithing is stealing. Stealing is *not* keeping God's commandments, and we should expect to receive accordingly.

Obviously, stealing is a bigger sin, and not tithing is a bigger problem, than most people have realized. And it is more widespread than you think.

There is a church in our city whose pastor has an eight-year-old daughter. After hearing her parents talk about church finances, the pastor's little eight-year-old decided she too wanted to put something in the church's offering plate. The very next Sunday she began making contributions out of her allowance. At the end of that year, while reviewing the church's finances, the pastor was shocked to discover his little eight-year old daughter had given more money to the church than over *one-third* of the adult congregation! (Read that a second time . . . .) That situation is extremely disappointing, and sadly reflects the state of giving in the church today. It blows my mind that an average of only 6 to 9% of Christians are tithing! 6 to 9%! But you can bet all 100% of Christians are praying and expecting results! It appears the "entitlement mentality" is alive and well in the Christian community.

Only when we put God first, release our grip on money and back our faith with performance, will our prayer lives begin producing miracles. You can take that to the bank. Pun intended.

You have to understand, and trust, that when it comes to your finances God would never ask you to do something that would put you in harm's way! Do you really think God wants you to go broke? No! Just the opposite! He *wants* you to do well! God wants you to be successful just as any parent wants their child to be successful. Contrary to the "poverty consciousness" that you may have been taught, God does not require that you drive an old car, wear tattered clothes or walk around with holes in your shoes! How could that possibly bring honor to Him? Ask yourself, as a parent, would you want that for your children? And if you did, how would that make you look to other parents? Make no mistake, God *wants* us to be successful and anyone who teaches you otherwise, quite frankly, has rocks in their head.

The only reason Bible-based prosperity falls under attack is because when God's Word improves a person's life, it makes God look good to the world, so the devil attacks it. It's that simple. Prosperity is a part of God's Word. So never let any person, or any religion, tell you otherwise. But for Bible-based prosperity to manifest itself in your life, you must live your life by Bible-based principles. And that includes your financial life as well.

Become an Honor Student

THE DICTIONARY DEFINES THE word "prosper" as a "successful outcome." That tells me that most people probably want to prosper. I mean, who doesn't want a successful outcome? Who wouldn't want a successful outcome from a surgery? Or a successful score on a math exam? Or a winning score in a football game? We all want successful outcomes! To think God wants His children to be unsuccessful is ridiculous.

God wants us to prosper so much that He tells us that *above all things* He wants us to prosper! It's in 3 John 1:2; look it up! And that verse doesn't say prosper in "some things." It says prosper in "ALL things!" In fact, in Deuteronomy 8:18, the Bible says it is God himself who gives us the *power* to get wealth, so that He may establish His covenant! This confirms that God doesn't object to successful outcomes financially, because wealth is one of the blessings He can use to establish His covenant! So for the members of the "holes in your shoes" crowd, if that doesn't get your attention, maybe this will. The Strong's Concordance indicates the Bible has 681 verses on prosperity, abundance and riches, but a mere 56 verses relating to "poverty and lack." 681 to 56! That's a 12 to 1 ratio in favor of living "with" as opposed to living "without!" That being the case, we need to accept that getting ahead financially and providing the best for our families doesn't make us greedy or sinful. Not at all. Especially since the Bible says it is God Himself who gives us the power to do just that. But with that having been said, if we want God's help in this regard, we must also learn to trust God with the finances we already have. Look, I'm sure you would agree that God is not a liar. So when God says He will pour us out a blessing and rebuke the devourer, why don't more believers tithe into their church? The answer is simple. Because they lack the very faith they profess to have, and lacking faith has never led to prayers being answered the way we want them to. There's an expression out there that says, "It takes a leap of faith." Well, if trusting God with your finances means taking a leap, do it! Take a deep breath and jump!

This is where it gets fun for God, because the day His children finally "take the leap" is the day they begin to grow, develop and to become successful. Psalm 35:27 says, "The Lord be magnified which hath pleasure in the prosperity of His servant." Have you ever seen those "My child is an honor student" bumper stickers?

Those bumper stickers are really saying two things. First, they're telling you that the parent is excited about the academic prosperity of their child. Secondly, they're telling you the parent is enjoying some "magnification" for themselves because of it. Sometimes I think the only difference between the God-parent, and the earthly-parent is that they don't have bumper stickers in heaven . . . (yet!).

If you are willing to work as hard as it takes to become financially prosperous, then put your attention on the One who controls the purse strings. And the One who controls the purse strings is God.

Pastors & Prosperity

Let me say this one last time. The last thing God wants for His children is to have them living unsuccessfully and going without. There's not a Christian parent alive who wants that for their children! Particularly for their most obedient children. This is where we need to talk about the most obedient children of all. The children called *pastors*.

Having grown up in a church of traditional religion, I was led to believe that a pastor had to be meek, soft-spoken and live a life without the luxuries the rest of us insisted upon. Basically, a pastor was supposed to live a lifestyle not too far above poverty. This lifestyle was apparently necessary to glorify God . . . ?

Really?

Who then, in their right mind, would want to get close to God? I mean, if that logic was true, then the child in a family who lives closest to the rules would be the child who must live with the least? Does that seem even remotely fair? Does it seem reasonable? Isn't that like saying the student who scores highest on the exam should get the poorest grade? Or the employee with the best performance gets the smallest paycheck? Clearly, this makes no sense. Since pastors live by God's rules more than anyone else, pastors should receive the best of God's blessings! The thought of this might fracture your religiously-framed perception of a pastor's life, but it is a logic that makes sense and a logic that the scriptures agree with. If you examine 1 Timothy 5:17, it says those who labor to spread the Word and doctrine should receive "double the wages."

Double!

Read it for yourself!

When it comes to finances, perhaps it's time to give your Christian perspective a chiropractic adjustment. Let's take it from the top. God, the Father Almighty, is so *Almighty* that He spoke the universe into existence with the sound of His voice. Then, He created you and me in His image, telling us that we can achieve the impossible! Then He sent His only son to earth who performed great miracles and who said that you and I could perform even greater miracles than He did! He also said that if we live by His rules and accept Jesus Christ as our Lord and Savior, we'd live an eternal life in a city made of *gold!* A city so luxurious that it's filled with gems, pearls and even has *streets* of gold! (You can look that up in Revelation 21:18-21.) He even taught us a prayer that states that His will should be done "on earth as it is in heaven." So if they have golden streets in heaven, and we are to have it on earth as it is in heaven, shouldn't we be building golden streets here on earth? Or at least be trying to? Clearly, we need to think more like God.

So I challenge you. Having been created in God's image and nature with the power to perform miracles and with a promise of a luxurious life surrounded by gold and gems, why would God set up a model for life on earth where His most obedient children live just a few steps above squalor? Particularly when the Bible says over and over that God is a "rewarder" to those who seek Him! (Hebrews 11:6) It makes no sense!

Welcome to God's Word without the limitations!

Pressuring pastors into living quiet, frugal, little lives is of no benefit to God. Separating pastors from financial success limits a pastor's ability to be charitable, and the pastor certainly can't give money to people who need money if the pastor has no money to give! So ask yourself, why are we painting pastors into such tight corners when pastors are God's most obedient children? It's not only ridiculous, but it's also bad marketing. It's bad marketing for the church, and it's bad marketing for God. And you'll never convince me God intended it to be that way.

Think about it. Pastors are the closest people to God, right? And why do we go to church? So we also can get closer to God. So if going to church brings us closer to God, and getting closer to God means that our families will have to live with less and less, eventually living with little at all . . . why would anyone go to church?

They wouldn't!

Rest assured, that is not God's plan. He didn't create us in His image with an unlimited potential to perform miracles, or promise us a city of gold, and then expect us to live a life on earth so unimpressive that His own children would flee from Him. God did just the opposite. God instructed us to *use our gifts* and let our lights shine! We're supposed to glorify God through our good works, and to live a life so bright and so abundant that when others see what we have, they'll want it for themselves! *That* is what brings people closer to God, brings lost children home their father and ultimately grows God's kingdom.

Take the Chains off Your Imagination!

Every one of us has the power to make miracles happen and to live a life so bright that other people will be drawn to the spirit inside of us. It is a life of God-given power, kindness, prosperity and greatness. It is the life that brings honor and glory to the Father who created us.

So if bright lights, miracles and prosperity is the model that brings people closer to God, where do we find the path to make that happen? The answer is simple. It's inside your imagination right now. Want me to prove it? Go find a quiet place and spend some time alone with God. If you have a prayer closet, go in and close the door. Ask Him to show you the visions He has for your life. Then, sit quietly, listening with your mind, and watch the visions begin to appear. As we mentioned earlier, pay particular attention to the visions that touch your heart with *desire!* Feel the *thrill* and pay attention to it! These are the visions that are in alignment with the talents and abilities you've been blessed with. Believe this! I said it before and I'll say it again, God wouldn't give you a desire-filled vision without also having given you the talent to make it real! That would be setting you up to fail, and failure doesn't bring glory to God. Winning does! And *winning* is what we are born to do. Check out 1 Corinthians 9:24, and you'll see that God wants you to capture the trophy! God wants you to win in every area of your life!

Striving to win seems natural when you're pursuing God's desire-filled visions for your life. Unfortunately, too many people are struggling to identify these visions, or worse yet, they've given up trying altogether! If this sounds like you, don't sweat it. The visions are still there, they're just buried under the limitations that have been laid over your thinking. But hey, no need to worry. We can take care of that right now.

Get a pencil and a sheet of paper and let's have some fun.

Imagine that you have all the time and all the money in the world. It is more time than you could ever use and more money than you could ever spend! Now ask yourself, given the fact you now have unlimited resources, what would you want for yourself and for your family? Go ahead, let your imagination run wild! Take your time with this and create perfectly clear images of what you want. Think about it carefully.

In a world of unlimited potential, what do you want your life to look like? What would you spend your life doing? If you could work your dream career, what would it be? I'm not talking about the career someone else is pushing you into, I'm talking about the career that was so exceptional that someone probably laughed you out of trying. Remember it now?

Think about how you would spend the fruits of your labor. What would you enjoy providing for your wife and for your children? What kind of home do you see yourself and your family living in? Is it a home in the city or country? Perhaps in the mountains? Maybe you'd enjoy a lake home? If so, be specific about it. Would it be a log home? Would your log home have a fireplace? Is the fireplace made of brick or stone? Do you prefer the fireplace to be gas or wood burning? And what about a boat to go skiing and tubing behind? Yes or no? And if yes, what color is it? Maybe you'd prefer a bass boat for fishing?

Now ask yourself, doing what you are doing now, are you putting all your gifts to use? Are you working your dream profession, or an 8 to 5 job you found online? And let me ask you this. Is doing what you're doing now able to provide your family with all the things you just got done listing? I'm asking these questions to kick-start your dreaming again! Because when you are working the career that God has designed you for and you are making use of the God-given talents He has blessed you with, all things become possible and your prayers become more efficient. Remember the fish climbing a tree? Stop being the fish, start being you, and THINK BIGGER!

As you've just discovered, letting your imagination run free can be fun! It can also be intimidating because God's visions for our life are much more grand than the "little pictures" we paint for ourselves. God created the entire universe! So yes, He thinks in BIG pictures! Maybe that's why the Bible tells us to be "strong and of good courage." Because God's goals are big goals, and big goals take courage!

Now, let's take a look at that paper of yours. What did you write? Do your thoughts and desires reflect the greatness of God? Or, do your thoughts appear constrained by the limitations of earthly thinking? Perhaps you should try it again and get serious this time. You need to accept this challenge and write down the visions God shows you! Then read them *out loud* every single day. You don't have to take just my word for this. The Old Testament, in Habakkuk 2:2, tells us to: "Write the vision, and make it plain upon tables [your sheet of paper] so that he may *run that readeth it*." Do you see why you must write it down? Because God's Word says the person who writes the vision and "reads" it begins to *run!* When you begin to run, it means you have engaged in performance. In other words, "works" have begun. Your God-given gifts are now in use, and God's Word says you will be blessed in your doing!

Look at it this way. If it was Christmas, are you the child who uses their gifts? Or are you the child who leaves their gifts laying under the tree?

Well, which is it?

It's time to knock the dust off your toys! Come on, get busy! Use your gifts! Generate some *works!* It will make God happy and help to justify the additional gifts and blessings we ask Him for when we pray! How do we know God sees it this way? Because we're all made in His image and nature, and we want our children using the gifts we've given them! So recapture your vision and get to work! You will be so glad you did!

All that being said, and all that excitement being generated, no conversation about prayer, visions or purpose is complete without mentioning the baptism of the Holy Spirit and the speaking of spiritual languages. For some reason, speaking in spiritual languages is a subject that is avoided more than even the subject of tithing. As a believer who accepts every Word of God to be true, this is extremely concerning. But, if you want to tell God how you don't think everything He says in the Bible is true, go right ahead. You have free will. But do you really think calling God a liar is going to have a positive influence on your prayers?

While I've certainly seen my share of people "faking" their way through spiritual languages (which

I believe to be a sinful and dangerous mocking of the Holy Spirit, so stop it if you're doing it), I also believe avoiding the subject is just as sinful. Let's take a quick look at just a few scriptures related to this practice.

The Bible is filled with verses on speaking in spiritual languages. So much so that every wedding I've ever attended has included 1 Corinthians 13:1 as a scripture reading. This scripture states: "Though I speak with tongues of men and of angels but have not love . . . ."

"Tongues of angels?" Yep, that's a spiritual language, and you probably used this verse in your own wedding! I'm pointing this out because I'm trying to get your attention. I hope it worked. Let's keep going.

Mark 16:16-17 tells us: "And these signs will accompany those who *believe*: by using my name they will cast out demons; they will speak in *new languages* . . . ." As you can see, these abilities apply to those who "believe." That means that if you are a believer, you too have the capacity to speak in *new languages*. This subject gets even more significant in the arena of prayer. In Romans 8:26 we learn that if we get caught in a jam and don't know what to pray for, the Holy Spirit will step in and assist us with our prayer. Romans 8:26 states, "Likewise the Spirit helps us in our weakness; for we do not know how to pray as we ought, but that very Spirit intercedes with sighs too deep for words."

"Sighs," sometimes referred to as "groanings," are spiritual language.

Certainly there is comfort in knowing that when we don't know what to do or what to pray for, the Holy Spirit will come to our rescue by interceding and doing our praying for us. Why anyone would turn their backs on this type of spiritual support is truly a mystery.

When it comes to your imagination, putting your gifts and talents to use, and understanding how it all fits into God's grand plan, no other chapter in the Bible is more exciting than 1st Corinthians 2. Throughout the second chapter of 1 Corinthians we find verse after verse of the significance of spiritual languages and how they help us tie it all together. In this chapter, we learn in verses 9-10 that none of us through our *human senses* have seen, heard or felt, what God has prepared for us. God's plan is only made known "through the Spirit." These verses tell us: "What no eye has seen, nor ear heard, nor the human heart conceived, what God has planned for those who love Him, these things God has revealed to us *through the Spirit*." Then, in verses 12-14, we get the clearest and most spectacular picture of all.

"Now we have received not the spirit of the world, but the Spirit that is from God, so that we may understand the gifts bestowed on us by God. *And we speak of these things in words not taught by human wisdom but taught by the Spirit,* interpreting spiritual things to those who are spiritual. Those who are unspiritual do not receive the gifts of God's Spirit, for they are foolishness to them, and they are unable to understand them because they are *spiritually discerned*."

What these verses tell us is that God's plan for us and the gifts He has given to those of us who are spiritual are not revealed at a human level or even in words taught by "human wisdom." God's grand plan for each of us who love Him is *taught by the Spirit*, and is *spiritually discerned*. That makes getting baptized in the Holy Spirit and being able to pray in spiritual languages an essential practice if we are ever to understand God's ultimate plan for our life. That means taking the chains off your imagination and embracing the full and uncompromised Word of God.

Vision Killers

One of the problems you'll have when traveling the road of your vision is staying focused on *your* vision and not ending up chasing someone else's. This happens when you put your attention on someone else's journey and take the focus off your own. It can also happen when someone else, like a parent, chooses the vision they want a child to pursue instead of supporting the vision God has chosen for the child. This happens all the time, and causes fortunes worth of gifts to go unused. This isn't just a problem for the person working toward the wrong vision. It is also a problem for the person who caused it to happen. Pay attention . . . .

Suppose you have a son who enjoys music. He is excited about playing the piano and dreams of someday playing in huge concert halls! How cool that your son knows *exactly* what he was put here to do! The only downside to his dream is that pianos are expensive, and so you'll need to find a second job to ensure that your son's dream becomes real.

After several months of working evenings with your second job, you've finally saved enough money to buy the piano for your son. You're feeling pretty large about life, and on the way to the music store you find yourself as excited as your son is! You buy the piano and the delivery truck follows you home. That evening your son plays the piano late into the night, refusing to go to bed. Even though it's a school night, you let him keep playing as you're admittedly enthralled with your son's extraordinary ability to play! No, he's not ready for Orchestra Hall yet, but he's playing at a level that far exceeds that of a typical first-day piano player. It is at this moment you realize that your son, truly, has been gifted from the Lord.

The next morning your son races over to a friend's house to share his excitement about his new piano. Unfortunately, when he gets there, he runs into his friend's father who isn't impressed with the piano at all. In fact, he laughs about the piano, rubbing in how he just bought his son a new motocross bike. The father wants his son to start racing motorcycles because it's a "man's sport" and tells your son that piano playing is for "sissies." He also tells your son how nobody ever makes any money playing music and how children who grow up wanting to become musicians are wasting their time.

Your son returns home with his feelings badly hurt. Later that afternoon you notice he hasn't played his new piano all day. When you ask him about it, he says he doesn't want the piano anymore. Your heart sinks when you hear the disappointed tone in his voice. That's when your son explains how his friend's father laughed at him about the new piano, and now he's afraid other people will laugh too. He no longer wants the piano and says he's sorry you ever bought it for him. All of your extra hours of hard work to pay for the piano have just become a giant waste of time and money. You become furious with the other father, and for good reason.

Five minutes later your phone rings. It's the other father calling you to borrow your truck. What do you think your answer will be?

How many of us at one time or another have laughed, mocked or discouraged, other people from pursuing a dream? How many times have we told someone they are too skinny, too fat, too small, too slow or that their "dreams are crazy?" Too many times, that's how many! What's even worse is, in the example we just reviewed, the little boy who got the motocross bike from his dad never even wanted a motocross bike! He wanted an aquarium because he was excited about oceanography! But no, his dad didn't like that idea either. What's going on here is that the dad never achieved his own vision of racing motorcycles, so now he's forcing his vision onto his son. People like this are nothing more than vision killers who turn countless gifts into carnage, and just like you wouldn't borrow him your truck, God won't respond to him either. Why would He? Why would God give something to someone who is causing all of His "pianos" to go to waste? He wouldn't. And neither would you.

We all need to remember that we were put here for different reasons and with talents and abilities that differ from one another. So avoid, at all costs, being a vision-killing source of discouragement and darkness, and seek to become a source of encouragement and light! Do this, and maybe next time you call Him, God will let you borrow the truck.

Stay on Course and Believe!

WITH ALL THE DISCOURAGING words some people tell us, and all the distractions the world can place along our path, we must occasionally reevaluate the direction we're headed in. Are we moving in a direction God has chosen for us? Or are we moving in a direction someone else has chosen for us? We need to be honest about this because it has such a big effect on our prayer life. Living on God's intended path aligns our efforts with God's purpose, which dramatically influences the effectiveness of our prayer life. And given the size of the challenges that can come our way, effectual prayer can be a priceless asset.

It doesn't matter who you are or how much faith you have, every now and then a mountain rises up and tries to stop us from reaching our destination. These mountains can be big and intimidating, but God's Word can be big and intimidating also. God's Word says that, "Whosoever shall say unto this mountain, be thou removed and be cast into the sea, and shall not doubt in his heart, but shall believe that those things which he saith shall come to pass, he shall have whatsoever he saith." (Mark 11:23)

There are so many key points to this one scripture we could spend hours talking about it. But for the purpose of our discussion here, we need to pay attention to the words, "shall not *doubt* in his heart, but shall *believe* . . . ." The point is, when you are on God's chosen path and using the gifts He so lovingly blessed you with, you can speak to those mountains, and speak with *confidence*, knowing that God is right there with you. And when God is with you, no mountain can stand before you! So speak to your mountain with confidence and cast it down! Then move forward knowing the best outcome is at hand. Remember, God wants us to speak with so much confidence and with so much belief that He taught Abraham to actually "call those things which *be not* as though they were." In other words, once you have spoken to your mountain, follow it up with words that indicate the situation has already come to pass. Do this even *before* you begin seeing the intended result appear in the physical world, and be diligent to avoid using statements of doubt! Statements of doubt will defeat your prayers, so don't go around telling people your "prayer didn't work" just because your prayer wasn't answered on *your* timetable! God will answer your prayer on *His* timetable, which is always the *correct* timetable.

When a person publicly declares God has failed with their prayer, rest assured this prayer will be left unanswered. But it won't be God who has failed. God's Word is clear about this. The Bible says that when you come to God with a request, it will done onto you "according to your faith." (Mathew 9:28-29) Praying and doubting is *not* coming to God in faith! And praying and declaring failure is worse!

As we said earlier, if you search out James 1:6-8, it becomes ever so clear we must pray with confidence. "But ask in faith, never doubting . . . for the doubter, being double-minded and unstable in every way, *must not expect to receive anything* from the Lord." It doesn't get any clearer than that. But if this still hasn't sunk in, read Matthew 21:22. In this verse we are told, "All things we ask in prayer, believing, we shall receive." This is a very short verse, but also a very powerful verse. There are three words of significance found in this verse.

The first of these powerful words is the word "all." Please notice how the scripture doesn't say "some" things we ask in prayer. It says "all" things. The second word of significance is the word "believing." Notice how it doesn't say "doubting!" Finally, please notice the word "shall." This verse doesn't say that we "might" receive. It says that if you pray and believe, you *shall* receive! So stop praying and doubting!

Look at it this way. Suppose a friend asked if you would do them a favor and you told them, "Yes." Then, even though you had said "Yes," they went around telling people how they doubted you would live up to your word. How would you feel? Well, how do you suppose God feels when we walk around telling people that He won't live up to *His* Word?

I'll tell you how it makes Him feel: He doesn't like it very much!

Do you know how I know this? Because you and I are made in His image and nature, and we wouldn't like it either!

It should be getting obvious that our relationships here on earth can play a key role in understanding our relationship with God. As we learn to improve our relationships here on earth, we can in turn, learn to improve our relationship with God. So play by God's rules, walk the path He has placed in your heart, and believe! Do this, and you will soon see your prayers produce with abundance!

No Magic Fairy Dust

HAVING LEARNED WHAT WE have so far, we've already traveled a considerable distance across the prayer spectrum, and are getting ever closer to the place of "praying and believing." But before we can get there, we need to do a couple more things. The first of which is take a more detailed look at the act of "performance."

Performance is about "doing." It is a form of the "works" that the Bible says activates the power of our faith. This is an exciting step! Because it shows what a person's faith is really made of and separates the talkers from the doers!

We talked about this behavior way back at the beginning. Somewhere along the course of time, "waiting upon the Lord" became the practice of "praying and sitting." Or to be blunt, it became the practice of "praying and sitting on your fanny!"

Did anyone really think that would work?

Can you imagine a child asking a parent for something they wanted *really* bad, and then the child just sits on their butt playing video games, waiting for it to be handed to them? Unfortunately, a lot of Christians have been taught to do the exact same thing with their prayers. They follow up a prayer request by sitting idle, putting forth no effort in the direction of what they are asking for! They pray. They sit. They do nothing.

News flash! Parents enjoy seeing their child "work" toward what they are asking for! God is no different! He also enjoys seeing you "work" toward the things you are asking for! So, after you make a prayer request, perform an action in the direction of your request! Show God how bad you want what you're asking for!

EARN your miracle!

The Bible clearly validates the process of praying and working. In the book of James (2:17, 22, 24, 26) we are told repeatedly that "faith without works, is dead." Again, notice the wording in the Bible. It doesn't say that faith without works is *weak*. It doesn't say that faith without works is *limited*. The Bible says that faith without works is *dead!* It couldn't be more clear. If you want your prayers to produce more horsepower, it is essential that your prayers are followed by "corresponding action." You must pray, and then *perform!* And then keep your eyes and your ears open!

So many people pray their prayers but never stop to consider the method through which the answer will be delivered! Seriously. Have you ever stopped to think about it? Do you think the answer will arrive on big, white, puffy cloud? Perhaps in the sprinkle of some magic fairy dust? Via email maybe? Perhaps on a banner being towed behind a small airplane? Okay, sarcasm aside, God can deliver an answer to your prayer any way He wants, so pay attention to your surroundings. Quite often He will deliver the answer right through the mouth of the person standing next to you! Whether it's a direction we need to take, a product we need to buy or a person we need to contact, God will provide the answer we've prayed for. Unfortunately, we too often miss it because we're looking for "magic fairy dust" when in reality, the answer was just spoken right to our face! That's why keeping your eyes and your ears open is so important. If you don't, you'll fail to realize that the person you just talked to, the article you just read or the billboard that just caught your attention, gave you the answer! So be attentive! Then, once you get the answer, engage in a corresponding action that is in alignment with the instructions you've been given! This "action" will generate momentum toward the desired outcome, and as you will see when you put this into practice, the success of your prayers will have risen to an entirely new level.

Let the Sweat Begin!

THERE'S ONE FINAL STEP to praying and believing, and to be honest with you, it can be the most difficult step of all. This final step is called "endurance."

Endurance requires both hard work and exhausting levels of patience. But what makes the word "endurance" so important in all of this is that it confirms that we must *expend effort*. It validates that we must put forth *works* as part of the process, which as we have just learned, is required to breathe life into our *faith*. When we pray with faith, we must be willing to show God how much we want something. That can mean working longer and harder than we expected, sometimes even to the point of exhaustion. Let me give you an example.

During the years I trained for my black belt, I pushed myself to the point of exhaustion (and even beyond) several times. I suffered countless bruises, bloodshed and even broken bones . . . whatever it took to achieve success. That was okay though, because if a person isn't willing to push themselves to the point of exhaustion and sometimes even beyond, they aren't learning the principles of *endurance*. And as much as we may not enjoy the pain of this process, there is a peace in knowing that by doing so, God will reward us in the end. This truth is validated in the book of Galatians (6:9) where we are told "not to be weary in well doing: for in due season we *shall* reap, if we faint not." The word "faint" used in this context is defined as "quit."

Once again, check the wording used. God's Word doesn't say, "we maybe shall reap." It says "shall" reap. This should give you confidence that when you pray with faith, work hard and endure, your prayers *will be answered,* if you don't quit! So go ahead, show God your winning effort, and God will show you *His!*

Now, before we go any further, let's take a quick review of what we've covered so far, and then we'll look at some real life examples that prove what we're saying is the real deal.

First of all, erase your chalkboard! We must all learn to forgive and forget so that our hearts are renewed and ready to love again. Without this, this is all a waste of time. So now that your heart is renewed, love God with all of it! Make God *"first"* in your life! When you wake up in the morning, you should joyfully declare, "Good morning, God!" Then, read from your Bible (out loud whenever possible), *before* reading from the newspaper or the internet. Next, talk to God through prayer before getting on your cell phone! This eliminates the pattern of only calling God when you need Him for something!

While driving, turn your car into a "Rolling University!" Faith comes by hearing and hearing! So spend as much time as possible listening to faith-filled CDs and other forms of Christian broadcasting!

Also, be sure to be thanking God as often as possible, and give Him the praise He deserves!

Then there are your gifts. Be sure they are getting put to good use *before* you start asking God for more, and absolutely, positively take care of your temple!

Then there's the big one. The one that gives people the touch of the devil . . . "tithing." If you want God to give your life and your finances a supernatural blessing, you have to defeat the love of money! That is *not* an option. "Sow" into your church so that you will reap at harvest time!

Finally, it is essential that you align your goals with God's purpose for your life! Then, move forward with *endurance*. Be willing to show God your winning effort! Do it! And you will soon see your prayers producing the fruit you were believing for! This will finally bring you to the place of "praying and believing."

Now for the moment you've been waiting for. Let's explore some real-life examples of what we've been learning that will bring all of this into perfect clarity.

A MIRACLE WIN

IF YOU WANT TO see the manifestation of miracles and the power of following God's calling on your life, this story will serve as an example you will never forget!

When I was a little boy, all I thought about was racing NASCAR. This wasn't just a phase I was going through. It was a powerful, non-stop vision for my life. And even though it brought laughter from more people than I have fingers and toes to count with, the vision to race NASCAR endured it all. Finally, long into my flying career, my dream of racing NASCAR eventually came to life!

I will never forget the thrill of taking my first "green flag." For those of you who don't follow NASCAR, the waving of a green flag is what starts the race. It is extremely exciting! It works like this. As the start of a race approaches, all of the cars out on the track begin bunching up tightly together, literally door-to-door, bumper-to-bumper. Then, as the cars approach the front straightaway, a green flag waves and every driver hits full-throttle! The engines roar, the cars accelerate like bullets, and every driver fights for position as the cars dive into the first turn. It is a thrill that no words can describe!!

From the night of that first race, I knew this was, in fact, the place I was created to be. After so many years of distraction, I had finally found "home."

Unfortunately, because of my flying career and the travel that comes with it, my first three seasons of racing were only part-time. But coming into the fourth season there was a lighter flying schedule so my mechanic and I decided it was time to put some trophies on the shelf. We made a decision to hit it hard that fourth season, and after some long hours and hard work, we won our first race! It was an eight lap shootout called a "heat" race. It was an experience I will never forget! Accelerating out of the final turn, with other cars just inches behind, I hit full throttle and began to realize that what I was seeing through the windshield was the real-life manifestation of a vision that had played in my mind since childhood: a vision of speeding down a straightaway in front of cheering fans and a checkered flag waving furiously as I sped by for the win! My boyhood vision was about to become real. And it did! It was absolutely breathtaking!

I will never forget returning home and placing that first trophy on the mantle next to my mother's picture.

I was able to choke out the words, "This one's for you, mom," before breaking into tears. Mom had become a race fan, and I knew in my heart she had been watching the race from heaven.

It was a blast having finally won my first race, but that didn't mean my racing career was over. To truly solidify the vision, I wanted to win more than a heat race. I wanted to win something called a "feature" race. A feature race is a bigger race with more cars and twice as many laps. Plus, the trophies are larger and there's more money to win. This makes for more competition, requires more concentration and has many more variables to conquer. To win a feature race would be huge! But that is when the bottom fell out of my race season.

The engine that was in the racecar was getting tired and losing power. I had no choice but to invest the money for a new one. This is an expensive decision and requires a significant amount of work. The old engine and transmission would have to be removed from the car. Then, the transmission would have to be separated from the old engine, fitted to the new engine, and then together, installed back into car. This was actually a much bigger project than it sounds like, because all the regular weekly maintenance still needed to be done and there was hardly enough time for that!

The new engine arrived. Although there were high hopes for the new engine, those hopes quickly dissolved as the following weeks became a total disaster.

Everything you can imagine was breaking on the new engine. We couldn't finish a race! It was one long night of repairs after another, until the new engine finally blew into pieces and sent me spinning out of control. Things couldn't have been worse. The amount of time and money we had spent on this engine project was ridiculous, and now the engine was destroyed! To make things even more frustrating, the mechanic who had been helping me all summer had bought his own racecar, which left me to finish the season without any help!

So, there I was. Exhausted, all alone and with a new engine blown to bits and leaking oil all over the ground. There were still two races remaining in the season, but that didn't matter anymore. This race season had just come to a very expensive and disappointing end.

After calling the engine builder to let him know the new motor was now junk, I found a couple guys to help me push the broken racecar onto the trailer and headed for home. I backed up to the garage, pushed the car off the trailer and closed the garage door. It was now 11:30 p.m. on a hot, humid Thursday night. The race season, for me, was over.

I went into the house and sat alone in my living room. I was beyond tired, dripping in sweat and smelled of car exhaust and motor oil. The brightly colored racecar that had made my boyhood dream a reality was now parked in a dark garage with its broken engine block dripping the last of its fluids onto the garage floor. The only thing on my mind was whether or not I should take a shower and go to bed or just fall asleep in the chair I was sitting in. That was when my mind came alive with the memories of the summer. Memories of the racetrack's announcer taking time to promote my book to the fans and how that had brought so many children to our pit slab after the races. We had so much fun letting the kids sit in the racecar for pictures while talking to them about their dreams. In fact, whenever a child would promise to never let anyone talk them out of their dream, we'd let them sign their name on the racecar! It was like having them sign a contract, except in this case the contract wasn't a sheet of paper. It was a racecar!

And then there was my friend, Rylee. The young woman racer who I had promised to let drive the car before the summer was over. I never break my promises! But with the car's engine blown, it looked like I was about to. The thought of breaking this promise was tormenting me.

So there I sat. Exhausted and alone with a head full of memories and a promise I wasn't going to keep. Clearly, I'd had better days . . . .

With my eyelids getting heavy and beginning to close, I was jolted by the words, "Prove what you preach!" Then, as though being lifted by the belt loops, I was on my feet and heading into the garage. I opened the toolbox, flipped up the hood of the racecar and began unhooking cables, unbolting exhaust pipes and loosening radiator hoses in preparation of removing the racecar's broken engine. Falling asleep in the living room chair was apparently no longer an option. Sleep would have to wait.

As the sun began to rise on Friday morning, I got in my truck and drove to a store to rent an engine lift. Getting the lift home and into the garage made it possible to remove the broken engine block and transmission. Next, I gathered up all the old engine parts that had accumulated in my garage and began assembling them into another race engine.

Times passed. It was now Friday night. I needed sleep, badly, and headed to bed for the next four hours.

As the sun rose Saturday morning, I was already in the garage working feverishly to assemble engine parts, align clutch plates, bolt down cylinder heads and install intake and exhaust manifolds. The details seemed endless!

It was at this moment I realized something *supernatural* was occurring. With only two races remaining there was nothing in my natural mind so urgent that it would push me to work at this machine-like pace. Furthermore, the old parts and pieces I was assembling into an engine wouldn't produce much power and would be lucky to withstand even a single night of racing! So what was I doing this for? The announcer? The kids? My friend Rylee? Did they matter to me? Of course they did! They were on my mind constantly while I worked. But something else was pushing me. Something extremely powerful! First Corinthians 15:10 says, "I worked harder than any of them, though it was not I, but the grace of God that was with me." As you'll see by the end of this story, this scripture had clearly come to life.

Later that morning the replacement engine was finally together. I carefully lowered it into the racecar and attached the motor mounts. After attaching the drive shaft, throttle linkage and dozens of other items, the engine installation was finally complete.

With the battery charged and the cables connected, it was time to start the engine and set the timing. I hit the power switch, pushed the start button, and the engine turned over. And over . . . and over . . . but it wouldn't start! It didn't even fire! Time and again I tried to start the engine, but time and again, it failed too.

It was now early Saturday evening. Frustrated and at a standstill, I prayed the words, "Father, help me." To which He replied, "Be humble."

So, humble I became. I made a phone call to another driver's mechanic named Randy. I had gotten to know Randy from being around the racetrack. He's a great guy, but the fact is, he would have no reason to help me. I race against his driver, which makes me a competitor, so of all the people in the world, why would he bother helping me? Besides, it was Saturday night and he was probably working feverishly to get his own car ready! But, Randy was a world-class talent with a wrench in his hand and I desperately needed his help, so I went for it and called him.

It was a night of God's favor. Randy said he would help and patiently spent the next 45 minutes talking me through a troubleshooting process, and then taught me how to set the cam timing.

Holding my breath, I pushed the start button again. The engine began to turn, and then with a mighty roar, it *started!*

Praise the Lord!

Sunday afternoon arrived. I was tired, pale, in a bit of daze and had one of those "dull" headaches that a whole bottle of aspirin wouldn't kill. Clearly not the best of days to go racing, but at this point, nothing was going to stop me.

I arrived at the racetrack to stares of disbelief. The guys at the track knew that my engine had just blown apart. They also knew I was racing alone without the help of a mechanic. They were so perplexed by the quick return of the racecar that even the racetrack's announcer, Kevin, was speechless (a rare event for a professional talker). Speaking of the racetrack's announcer, I was glad that he had stopped by the pit slab. It gave me a chance to honor him by explaining how the attention he puts on the racecar had played a big role in getting the car back together so quickly. It was also the first chance I'd had to show both himself and the fans that what we "preach" isn't just a bunch of talk, but that it is "real."

Next, I explained to my friend, Rylee, how she too was a force in getting the car back to the track so quickly. I had made her a promise and intended to keep it. Breaking promises does not glorify the Lord! *Keeping* promises does.

At this point, everything that was propelling this event to unfold was based on other people, how those people might possibly be influenced, and how all of this might reflect on the Lord. None of this had anything to do with myself or my own desires.

The afternoon pressed on. There were two races to be run, the first of which was a heat race. In the heat race the car had a reasonable run, finishing mid-pack and incurring no damage. It was a bit later, before the start of the feature race, that this story would truly begin to unfold.

While preparing the car for the feature race, Randy (the mechanic) walked up to me and said, "If you can get out front, you can set your sail." These were important words to be placed into my thinking, because the night of my first and only win, which was a heat win earlier in the summer, had proved to be the smoothest I had ever driven. It had reminded me, literally, of sailing. When Randy spoke the words "set your sail" it brought my thinking back to that night, and the memories of being "smooth."

Then, with the feature race drawing ever closer, another driver walked up, looked me straight in the eye and said, "Robert . . . smooth." It was at that moment I knew the Holy Ghost was speaking to me through other drivers. Then something else happened. When the lineup for the race was posted, the racetrack computer had randomly selected to put me up front in the pole position (front row, inside). This is the premiere place to start a race! The fly in the ointment, however, was that a former class champion was starting right alongside me in the "outside pole" position. As a former champion, he knew all the tricks to a good start, and his car had a much newer engine. An engine with substantially more horsepower than the assembly of spare parts that were bolted together under my hood!

The announcer called for our cars to line up for the feature race. I began my pre-race prayer, asking God to watch over me and keep me safe, to please help me run fast and clean, and honor Him in all that I do.

The racecars began to roll . . .

With the start of the race approaching, the cars bunched up tightly together and the green flag waved! The drivers all hit full-throttle and accelerated as hard as we can! Just as I had suspected, my car was underpowered and the former champion began to pull ahead in the outside lane. Into the first turn, the champion's car was faster, but mine was handling better, and I stayed with him through the turn. Down the back straightaway, the former champion inched ahead. Through another turn, I hung close. After two laps, the champion was more than a car length ahead of me, but staying high in the outside lane. I was expecting him to drop down in front of me, but he wasn't making the move. I was fighting as hard as I could to stay with him, knowing that if his car got down in front of mine, the race would be over!

Then, out of my memory come the words, "Robert . . . smooth." (Advice I had already forgotten!)

"Don't push it." I said to myself. "Smooth."

Just as it was during the heat win earlier in the season, the smoother I drove, the faster my car was traveling!

Another lap and I had closed the gap on the leader. One more lap and I was alongside of him. A few moments later, and he was in my mirror! The smoothness had paid off! I was leading the feature race!!

Then came the words, "Set your sail." The Holy Ghost had spoken. I set my sail . . . driving more smoothly than I had ever driven before, hitting all my marks, and the racecar was flying! Then, reality. "Stay humble." There were several other racecars out on the track, and every driver wanted to win just as badly as I did! This race was far from over. "Concentrate, and stay smooth," I kept telling myself.

Bang! My concentration broke. Coming into the turn off the front straightaway, another car had hit my left rear corner. My car broke loose and began to slide sideways. A gentle counter-steer to the right, the car responded to the correction, and we were straight again. I hit the gas, full-throttle, and I was still in the lead!

Racing down the back straightaway with less than two laps to go, I looked up through the windshield and yelled to the Lord, "Stay with me Buddy!!"

You heard me correctly . . . I called the Lord, "Buddy."

Down the front straightaway the white flag waves. One lap to go! STAY SMOOTH! Into turn one, just a brush of the brake, through the apex, full-throttle coming out of turn two. Down the back straightaway, maximum rpm, then into turn three. STAY SMOOTH! A brush of the brake, through the apex, full-throttle out of turn four. A quick glance in the mirror. Two cars close behind! One of them on my bumper, the other off my right quarter panel, but neither were closing! I turned my attention back to the front straightway wanting to absorb *every second* of this! "Is this really happening?" I thought to myself. My boyhood dream is coming true, today? On almost no sleep? With just a bunch of old engine parts under the hood?

That is when it happened. For the first time in my life the Lord made His "presence" known to me. What I'm about to tell you is difficult to describe with words, but I'll do my best.

Manifesting into the passenger side of the racecar's interior, up by the dash and looking back at me, was the presence of the Lord. It was unlike anything I'd ever felt before. No, I couldn't *see* Him. But I could *feel* Him. So much so, that I could tell He was facing my direction, looking at me. Then, right in the middle of all the noise, speed and excitement, I heard Him say:

"You know I'm here, right?"

To which I replied, "I do."

The Lord said, "This isn't about you."

At that moment the checkered flag waved with fury!! We won!!

Never before had the scripture "Faith without works is dead" become more alive! Since my childhood I *knew* God wanted me chasing checkered flags, and it was finally happening! *This* is what I was created to do! And because I had kept my faith in His plan, and had powered my faith with "works," God rewarded me with a bigger win than I could have ever asked for! This win was a *full-blown miracle*, and I knew it . . . but remember, the Lord said it wasn't about me.

Holding the checkered flag high into the air I drove my first ever victory lap, and then turned the car into victory lane. WOW; what a feeling! As the car slowed to a stop a crowd of fans came running over to celebrate the win!

As I climbed out of the car amidst the cheering fans they were caught by surprise as I began shouting, "This wasn't about me! Someone's life was changed here tonight! . . . This wasn't about me! Someone's life was changed here tonight!" I shouted it over and over, and even shouted that they had "just seen a miracle!" What had just happened was a piece of God's handiwork, not mine, and I was doing everything I could to give God the praise He deserved!

In the moments that followed, as everyone was being positioned for the victory lane photo, something unexpected happened. A man walked up with a little girl and asked if she could hold my trophy in the victory lane photo. To be honest, I thought he was kidding! I had waited my entire life for this moment! But as I glanced down at the cute little girl I felt a "nudge" to give it to her. I think that "nudge" might have been God saying, "Didn't you hear what I just said a few minutes ago? Give it to her!" So, I handed the little girl my trophy, and she and I posed for the photo together.

What none of us realized at that moment was that the victory lane photo was going to be published in a local newspaper. What we also didn't realize was that the little girl holding my trophy had an estranged grandfather. A grandfather who had raced at this same track for several years. From what I understand, he had been a very talented racecar driver and had celebrated in victory lane many times. But for all his trips to victory lane, he had never celebrated with his cute little granddaughter. Sadly, he had rarely ever seen her.

The grandfather had fallen deeply into alcohol and gambling. It was an addictive and destructive lifestyle that had ended his racing, and had torn his family apart. Well . . . , tore it apart until our victory lane photo appeared in a local newspaper.

The week following the feature win, a man who knew the little girl's grandfather saw the photo in the newspaper. Then, on the next weekend, he saw the grandfather sitting in the grandstand at the racetrack! (A place where the grandfather hadn't been for years!) The man presented the newspaper to the grandfather, showing him his granddaughter's photo. The grandfather sat quietly, staring at the photo of his granddaughter celebrating in victory lane with a total stranger. After minutes of silence, the grandfather looked up and said, "Maybe it's time I clean myself up so my granddaughter can celebrate in victory lane with her grandfather." It was then that the man who brought him the newspaper, pointed the grandfather's attention to the other end of the grandstand. His entire family, including his granddaughter, was sitting just a few hundred feet away. Before the end of the evening, the grandfather, the granddaughter and the rest of the family were all watching the races, together.

The Bible says our visions are for "an appointed time." My vision for winning races validates this, as this was obviously for an appointed time. And that time wasn't on my timetable. It was on God's. It had to be because there was more going on "behind the scenes" than I realized. Yes, my vision of winning races had finally become real, but there were far more important elements needing to come into alignment first. A little girl needing to be reunited with her grandfather was one of them. I know in my heart there were others in attendance that night whose lives were also changed. More lives will be changed in the future, which is why we all need to follow God's calling on our lives—and on His timetable.

"I worked harder than any of them, though it was not I, but the grace of God that was with me." 1 Corinthians 15:10. Truly, this scripture had come to life.

These types of divinely inspired events serve to magnify a person's faith. They prove that when a person has the courage to follow God's plan for his or her life and backs their faith with works, visions become reality and miracles really do happen. But if this example of victory isn't enough to convince you, maybe this next story will. Hang onto your hats.

THE ANGELS ARE LISTENING

THREE WEEKS AFTER THE miracle win, I was out of town on a trip for work. While driving along on my way to dinner, as I often do, I was using the time alone in the car to pray. While in the middle of my prayer, I happened to notice the time. Obviously, I wasn't racing on this particular evening, but back home it was just about time for my friend, Rylee, to go out onto the track. Since I was already praying, I thought I'd take a minute and say my pre-race prayer for her. So, I asked God to please watch over my friend Rylee, to keep her safe, to help her to race fast and clean, and to honor Him in all that she does. Then, in an uncontrolled burst of emotion I began *pleading* to the angels to "release themselves at the speed of lighting," and go to Rylee and protect her! The prayer went on and on until tears streamed from my eyes and began dripping off my cheeks! I was being overwhelmed by something I couldn't identify. It broke me into a gut wrenching plea to the angels and had me rambling words that were beyond my control. Nothing like this had ever happened before in my prayer life!

Once this tear-filled rant had ended and a few minutes had past, I decided to try this same prayer again.

"Heavenly Father, please watch over my friend, Rylee, and keep her safe. Help her to race fast and clean, and honor you in all that she does." And then it happened again! I began pleading to the angels to "release themselves at the speed of lighting!!!!" My stomach wrenched. Tears flowed. I can't repeat the exact words I was ranting because I simply cannot remember what they were. This was an extraordinary experience, and having occurred twice in just a matter of minutes, I had no choice but to believe something *supernatural* was taking place. I just didn't know what it was or what it meant.

After a stop for dinner, I got behind the wheel of my rental car and headed back to the hotel. Just a few minutes into the drive, my cell phone rang. I answered the phone and heard the words, "Rylee had a bad crash!" (I almost drove off the road and into the ditch!)

The caller urgently began explaining how Rylee's car had spun sideways, flipped over onto its roof and had skidded down the track upside down.

"Enough about the crash!" I impatiently shouted. "Is she okay!!!"

"She's fine," the caller replied.

Admittedly in a bit of shock, I explained to the caller how just minutes earlier I had prayed for Rylee, and had broken into a tear-filled rant about angels releasing themselves at the speed of lighting! Ordinarily, I would have been uncomfortable mentioning such a thing, but the caller himself was there for my feature win and knew the story of the little girl and her grandfather. That being the case, I thought he would marvel at the realization that another supernatural event had just occurred.

When I got back to my hotel room, I immediately called Rylee. She confirmed that the crash had occurred, but thanks to God and the angels, she had emerged from the crash unharmed. It was during the phone call that the brutality of the crash began to unfold. Rylee explained how coming out of turn two and accelerating down the back straightaway, her car got sideways, possibly from being nudged by another car. Then, in an instant, the car violently flipped all the way over onto its roof, spinning and shooting sparks as it slid down the back straightaway. What makes the story even more terrifying, is that Rylee's helmet strap hadn't gotten fastened before the race, so when her car flipped over, the inertia from the flip pulled her helmet off her head! Rylee was left hanging upside down in her safety harness, with her head openly exposed, as her racecar went skidding down the racetrack on its roof. It gets worse.

In Rylee's class of racing, the racecars have a roll bar in the back of the car, but up along the windshield, in the front of the car, they don't. What that means is, while Rylee's racecar was on its roof and skidding down the straightaway, the car's roof was slowly collapsing onto Rylee's helmet-less head! Rylee explained how when she saw the roof of the car slowly collapsing, she tucked her chin down onto her sternum to make room between the top of her head and the collapsing roof of her racecar.

The racecar eventually skidded to a stop with all four tires pointed to the sky. The car's throttle had stuck wide open causing the engine to race at maximum rpm until it finally seized up and quit. Rylee's helmet was visible through the upside down passenger window, laying by itself, very clearly not on her head where it was supposed to be. The rescue workers sprinted to her car and peered in through the windows of the upside down racecar. They found Rylee dangling upside down in her safety harness, her blonde hair making contact with the sunken roof of the racecar. After bracing herself as best as she could, she unbuckled her harness, and clumsily tumbled onto the ceiling of her car. She then crawled out the window of the racecar and emerged unharmed. Praise the Lord.

The rescue workers helped Rylee climb up onto the bottom of her upside down racecar where she gave an "I'm okay" wave to the thundering applause and of her fans.

The angels had done their job.

Was anything about this story of prayer a coincidence? Not a chance. This story is so powerful it would give an atheist second thoughts.

A few days after the car crash, I asked Rylee if she had any second thoughts about getting back into her racecar. She told me if the safety crew could have flipped her car back onto its wheels, she would have finished the race! Impressed by her response, I asked Rylee where she gets her courage? She looked me straight in the eye and said, "Jesus Christ is my *force*."

Amen to that!

This story provides us an additional clue into the power of prayer. It is the power that occurs when praying *Christian to Christian*. In other words, when a Christian prays for another Christian, the person on the receiving end of the prayer is more likely to be "open to receive." Think of this person as having their "window" open. This is contrary to praying for a non-believer. In most cases, a non-believer's heart is "closed" to the possibilities of prayer. In other words, their window is "shut." The Bible says that what a person receives is done "according to their faith." So when the person we are praying for has no faith and doesn't want any faith, it becomes difficult for a prayer blessing to manifest. You need to know this for the confidence in your own prayer life, because even "believers" often pray, and are prayed for, with doubt in their hearts. "Doubting" and "believing" are polar opposites! This causes a person to become "double minded," and the Bible says that a double minded person will receive "nothing."

When a person prays, they must pray and "believe"! Hopefully, these last couple stories will have brought you into a position of doing so!

God Apparently Makes House Calls!

It is important to understand that your prayers are being heard, and that your personal circumstances are constantly in God's watchful and loving hands. This was never more evident than when writing this message on prayer. Allow me to explain.

Whenever I'm being called to present a message, I don't receive the entire message all at once. The message comes in pieces. First, I receive the general category (in this case, *prayer*). Then, I begin receiving specific details in what I believe is the sequence God wants them presented. This "one detail at a time" process has been so consistent that I've never actually known the end of a message at the time I began preparing it. I've learned that God will deliver what I need, when I need it, including the conclusion. This message on prayer has been no exception, but that doesn't make it easy or stress free! Imagine investing a calendar full of "midnight oil" evenings working on a project and all the while not knowing where it is going or how it will end. No one enjoys feeling like they're on a journey to nowhere. As much as I've learned that the Lord will provide what I need when I need it, there are still times when my stress level gets the best of me. Waiting for the conclusion of this prayer message was one of those times.

After investing months into this project, I ended up sitting idle, having *no idea* how to bring it to a conclusion. Frustrated, I went out for a drive hoping to reduce the stress and clear my head. It was a dark and rainy evening and after driving a while, I pulled into a roadside restaurant for a late night cup of coffee.

A sign inside the restaurant said, "Hostess will seat you." I stood inside the door for just a few moments and the hostess arrived to walk me into the restaurant. I plopped myself down into a booth and a waitress soon headed my way. She was a pleasant young brunette who, having arrived at my booth, flipped open her order tablet and said, "How are you this evening? What can I bring you?" To which I replied, "I'm fine, a cup of black coffee, and how are *you* doing this evening?" With a look of surprise, the waitress eagerly responded, "I'm fine, and thank you for asking! Nobody ever asks how *I'm* doing!" And that's why I said it! Because nobody ever asks waitresses how *they* are doing! (Try it some time!) It brings a smile to their faces and let's them know the service they provide is appreciated.

So, there I sat. All alone in the booth, quietly drinking coffee hoping to hear from God. Time was passing. I consumed a half-pot of late night coffee and still nothing. Eventually, I said good night to the waitress, drove myself home and turned in for the night.

Approximately 3:30 a.m. I awakened from my sleep and soon began tumbling back and forth, impatiently waiting to fall back to sleep. Selfishly, I decided that if I laid there and prayed for a few minutes, it might help me fall back to sleep. (Perhaps the worst motivation to pray I have ever heard of.) Bad motivation or not, I put the palms of my hands together and then slide them between the side of my face and my pillow. Basically, resting my head on my hands. Then, in a slow tired whisper, I began speaking these unenthusiastic and clichéd words: "Dear God, thank you for all that you do for us . . . ." Yep, lame. In fact it sounded so insincere that I actually apologized for the way in which it sounded.

"I'm sorry, God, that was really lame."

A few moments later, out from the stillness of night, I received one of the most significant communications of my lifetime. Coming down from the above the foot of my bed I hear the words, **"You never ask how *I* am doing."**

Startled, I flipped onto my back and sat up on my elbows. I couldn't see God, but I could feel His presence staring down at me. What made this comment so piercing was that it reflected the conversation I had with the waitress just a few hours earlier.

And after giving it some thought, I had to admit it, God was right. I *never* ask God how He is doing. Nobody does. Have you? It brought feeling self-centered and inappreciative to an all new and spectacular level. So, while still sitting up on my elbows in the darkness of my bedroom, this is what I told Him.

"You know God, you're right. We never ask about you. How *are* you doing? I mean really, you do so much for us. You've given us all that we have, and all that we will ever have. That's a lot. Do you ever get tired? I mean, you created the earth, the planets, the solar systems, and we know you are expanding the universe at this very moment. You *must* get tired, don't you? You must get tired because on the seventh day, you rested. You do so much for us Father. More than we can even imagine. And you even gave us your Son."

A pause of silence . . . then came the words:

"I-WATCHED-HIM-DIE."

At that instant, I jumped out of bed and headed for a pen and sheet of paper. It was now 3:46 a.m. The end of this prayer message was being delivered and I didn't want to miss a word!

With pen in hand, God spoke again, but this time adding more.

"I WATCHED HIM DIE, *FOR YOU*. AND STILL LEGIONS OF PEOPLE TURN THEIR BACKS ON ME."

Why did God say this?

Because it's true!

There is no cliché that cuts deeper than the scripture found in John 3:16, "For God so loved the world that He gave His only Son, so that everyone who believes in Him may not perish but may have eternal life."

We've recited those words so often that most people, even Christians, have lost total appreciation for the meaning behind them. We've also never stopped to consider the pain God endured as He watched His Son being beaten, tortured and killed, *FOR US*. God could have stopped the beating, ending the pain for His son, and for Himself. But He didn't! He endured all that pain, for you.

I once heard a preacher say that God wanted a relationship with us so much that He actually "enjoyed" watching His Son die. That's crazy talk, and if you've heard it, dismiss it. Do you have children? Could you have done what God did? Of course not. But if you could, how would *you* feel if the people you did it for turned their backs on you and walked away? THINK about it. Because we have very clearly determined that God has feelings just like you and I do.

God suffered the pain of watching His Son die for us, and in return, we make a cliché out of why He did it, and then shamefully turn away from Him. We deny Him at work because we're afraid of what our boss might think. We deny Him in our schools because we're afraid of what other parents might think. We deny Him among our friends because we're afraid of what our friends might think. And if you don't think you're guilty of some of this, perhaps the month of December and the words "Happy Holidays" will jog your memory.

Let me ask you something. How do you feel when your children deny *you*? Or when your children are embarrassed to have you around? Does it make you feel loved and appreciated? Of course not.

God feels the same way.

How do we know God feels this way? Because God made us in His image and nature, and when our children push us away, it hurts us also.

We turn away from God almost every day, unless of course, our heart gets broken, or a loved one gets sick, or we find a lump in our bodies. Then, in a flash, we turn right back to God! And do so expecting Him to answer our prayers in the way *we* want them answered and on *our* timetable!

I get worked up just thinking about this, so I'll take a deep calming breath and then take this in a different direction.

Ask yourself this. How do you feel when your children miss you and want to be close to you? Does it make you feel good or bad? How about when your children honor you in front of their friends, telling everyone how they have the best parents, ever!

How do you feel when your little son or daughter raises their hands to you, wanting to be picked up and held? Or when your little three-year old climbs up onto your lap to watch cartoons on a Saturday morning? Does it make you feel good when your child enters the room just to tell you they love you? It warms your heart, doesn't it?

When we come close to God, it pleases Him. When we honor God in front of our friends or when we tell God we love him, it touches God's heart and makes Him smile. How do we know this? Because we are made in God's image and it makes us smile!

There is no greater feeling than when a parent feels the love of their child. We need to show God that same love and give God that same feeling! Climb up on His lap and watch a cartoon if you have to, but make sure He knows how much you love Him! This isn't rocket science! When God *knows* you love Him over all other things, your prayers will take on an entirely new level of power. Absolutely guaranteed.

RESTORING HIS MAJESTY

ON THE SUBJECT OF love, there is another cliché we need to erase and erase quickly. We need to get away from the constant overuse of the word "love."

Never has a word lost its majesty like the word that represents all that God is. That word is "love." Scripture tells us that God himself *is* love. It is who He is. Love is how God connects Himself to each of us in this world. Love is also the most powerful source of energy that is available to humankind. It is the supernatural fabric that holds everything together, and yet we throw this word around with total disregard of its origin, its meaning and its majesty.

We are told in 1 John 2:15 to not love the things of this world. But listen to us! We love a car, we love a computer, we love a dress, we love a joke, we love a lamp, we love a chair, we love a movie and we love money. It has to stop! Since love is what God is, carelessly throwing the word "love" around is dangerously close to taking the Lord's name in vain. Using the word "love" should be your confession of the highest level of affection. But if you "love" your lamp and you love your spouse and you love your children and you love God, then you have just told your family and you have just told God, they mean as much to you as your lamp! This is belittling to your family, and it is belittling to God!

Learn to use the word "love" sparingly. Protect it and cherish it. You will learn to feel pleasure by holding the word "love" in reserve. Then, after the people around you learn the protective way in which you hold this word, when you do finally speak it to someone, the word "love" will carry the power it was intended to have. It will penetrate the human heart the way it was meant to, and create an intimate connection between you and the person you use it with. Most importantly, it will heighten your understanding of God and bring you closer to Him.

In restoring the majesty to all that love is, we magnify its brilliance. We restore its power, and reestablish the "majesty of God" into the forefront of our minds and our hearts. This is where God is supposed to be and where we are commanded to keep Him. Love is what creates the supernatural connection with God that produces the blessings, the endurance and the power to achieve all things. Knowing this, and more importantly, believing it, is absolutely essential to a productive and prosperous prayer life.

So here are the six simple things you can do to *pray with performance* and make miracles happen—miracles in *your* life and the life of your loved ones:

1. Erase your chalkboard. Forgive, forget and get all the anger, bitterness and distrust that is in your heart, out of your heart. Begin with a fresh heart that is ready to love.

2. Now that your heart is renewed, love God with all of it. Keep Him *first*. Read your Bible *out loud* and pray to Him first thing each morning. Then go the extra mile by turning your car into a "Rolling University." Faith comes by hearing!

3. Be thankful to God for *everything* and give praise to God every chance you get!

4. Take care of your body! Your body is God's temple!

5. Tithe! We cannot be stealing from God and expect Him to answer our prayers!

6. Follow the *fire of your heart* and put your gifts to use! Dare to take your journey!!

Remember always that *every* Word of God is true, and that faith without *works* is dead! So trust in the visions God shows you, and then show God you have the courage to perform! *Unleash* the life that is inside of you, pray every step of the way and watch the manifestation of miracles begin to appear. This is what it means to pray at *full throttle*. Go for it! And you too will find yourself in victory lane.

About the Author

Robert Bakke is a jet captain and aerobatic flight instructor; a black belt, karate instructor and regional champion; a ski instructor; a racecar driver; an author, and was running a multi-million dollar company by the age of 24. After managing sales of $1,000,000.00 to $3,000,000.00 per day and shattering numerous sales records, Robert eventually saluted good-bye to his business career and moved on to captain jet aircraft, teach the "performance" of God's Word and author books to help people reach their highest levels of achievement. Robert received his Certificate of Ordination as a Minister of the Gospel on April 15, 2012.